Let's Pretend!

Written by Kate Scott

Illustrated by Ashley Stewart

Collins

Dev dipped his foot into the pool, checking it was not too cold.

Jake slid in. "Jump in, Dev!" he cried.
He splashed and made little waves.

Dev waded over to Jake.
"Let's pretend we are swimming in the sea," he said.

Dev and Jake swam down. "Look over there," said Jake, pointing. "A sea snake!"

"What's that?" asked Dev.

"It's a cave," said Jake. "Let's take a look inside."

They entered the amazing cave.

Jake felt his way along in the dark.

Jake screamed. His hand was entwined in a string of seaweed.

The boys lifted the seaweed, to find a ...

9

"SQUID!" Dev screamed. "Swim for your life!"

The boys hurried out of the cave.
"It's got my costume!" Jake yelled.

Dev swam back to help Jake.

Dev needed a plan. He grabbed the seaweed and wound it round and round the squid.

Now the squid could not see. As it tugged at the seaweed, it let go of Jake.

"Quick! Swim!" Dev shouted.

Both boys swam away from the squid.
They didn't look back.

They swam near sea snakes, flounders,

a manta ray and some seals.

They didn't stop until they had reached the top.

"Hooray! That was fun!" smiled Dev.

Jake said, "Let's pretend next week, too!"

"Come on, Jake! Come on, Dev!" said their mums.

21

Pretending

🐾 Review: After reading 🐾

Use your assessment from hearing the children read to choose any GPCs, words or tricky words that need additional practice.

Read 1: Decoding
- Ask the children to find and read the words **find** and **life**, on pages 9 and 10.
- Ask the children:
  - Can you tell me which sound is the same in each word? (*/igh/*)
  - Can you point to the grapheme (letter or letters) that represent the /igh/ sound in each word? (*i, i-e*)
  - Can you think of any other words with the /igh/ sound in them? (e.g. *time, wild*)

Read 2: Prosody
- Model reading each page with expression to the children. After you have read each page, ask the children to have a go at reading with expression.
- On pages 5 and 6, show the children how you read the dialogue, miming the actions and using lots of expression.

Read 3: Comprehension
- For every question ask the children how they know the answer. Ask:
  - Where was the story set? (*in a swimming pool*)
  - Where did Dev and Jake pretend to be? (*in the sea*)
  - Can you remember some of the creatures they saw? (e.g. *manta ray, sea snake*)
  - Do you like to play "let's pretend"? Where do you pretend to be? What do you see and do there?